Caique Parrots

A Pet Guide for Caique Parrots

Caique Parrots General Info, Purchasing, Care, Cost, Keeping, Health, Supplies, Food, Breeding and More Included!

By Lolly Brown

Foreword

The caique parrot is a tiny bird with happy disposition and an outgoing personality. It is lauded as the "class clown" of the parrot family it falls under because of its fearless antics with comical results. The caique has a rambunctious and active personality which can be truly entertaining to watch. They possess beautiful colors which are distinct as they are stark. There are two sorts of caique's classified as major species and each of them have unmistakable coloration that is distinct from the other.

In terms of personality, both the caique parrots have little difference in their personalities and have the tendency to gravitate toward one family member more than the rest, however with proper socialization, it can get along well with the rest of the family and is truly loyal in every sense. The caique bird is an incessant player and has a penchant for constant frolic and play making them great house companions. Provide them with interactive toys and sundries which not only stimulate them physically, since they are highly intelligent birds it is very important that they get the mental stimulation they so need to thrive healthily as well. With its high activity level, the caique birds need to be kept engaged constantly, because you just wouldn't believe the amount of trouble a bored bird can bring about.

Get to know the characteristics and personality of the caique parrots before making a decision on bringing one home. Give yourself the opportunity to investigate every single thing you will need to know about these small, colorful birds that have a penchant for play and chatter. There is nothing more calming than the sounds of plants blowing gently in the wind along with the bird song of our avian friends. If you have enough space to house more than a couple of these colorful flyers then you are indeed one of the lucky ones. And a few colorful caiques is really a great addition to your spacious aviary.

Caique parrots are dexterous acrobats who enjoy looking at the world upside down as it hangs wrong side down on a swinging perch. In between its busy job of hopping from one spot of the cage or aviary to the next, it stops to drink and eat in between. It is a caiques joy to be provided with the provisions it would need to gather its energy which it quickly burns. For a teeny bird, when compared to its larger cousins, the caique bird is seen to be a normally hearty eater. Its food in consists mostly of fruits and grubs, we'll be letting you in on the sorts of foods you can serve up to your own caique birds at home. We will also be discussing the vitamins you will need to supplement its diet with as you read through the rest of the book.

Find utilitarian tips on what you need to look out for in terms of space that you would need to comfortably house one caique and how much area you would need to raise a couple or more. Caique parrots do on their own or in pairs, discover if they are able to get along well with other avian birds you may already have.

Table of Contents

Introduction..1

A Profile of the Caique Parrot 1

Quick Stats on the Caique Parrot 3

Chapter One: General Description and Distribution 9

Types of Caique Birds 10

White - Bellied Caique 10

Black - headed caique 11

Determining Caique Parrot Gender 12

Lifespan of the Caique Parrot 13

Chapter Two: Choosing a Caique Parrot...............................15

Adopting a Caique 17

Bird Sanctuaries 18

Caique Breeders..18

Health of the Caique...19

Chapter Three: Maintaining Wellness of the Caique Bird ...21

Proper food and feeding schedules 22

Maintenance of enclosure.......................................25

Chapter Four: Required Space, Enclosure and Sundries......27

Housing Requirements 28

Bird Housing, Toys, Playpens and other Equipment.....29

Housing and Bird Cages: 30

Aviary **31**

Chapter Five: Breeding a Caique Parrot 33

Breeding Basics **34**

Things you want to keep in mind before the breeding
season starts 36

Breeding and Breeding Environment **38**

Egg Laying and Hatchlings: **39**

Incubation **41**

Breeding Caique Parrot Laws in the United States **42**

Chapter Six: Kids and Parrots 45

Reminders When Keeping Parrots **46**

Chapter Seven: Hygiene and Nutrition of the Caique Parrot
.... 51

Caring for and Feeding Your Caique Parrot: **52**

Bird Food and Formulated Diet **53**

Seed Diet **54**

Grooming Your Caique Parrots **54**

Bird Baths **55**

Wings **56**

Beak **56**

Nails **57**

Chapter Eight: Bird Proofing Rooms and Training Your
Caique 59

Bird Proofing Your House 60

Training and Handling Caique Parrots 64

Taming Basics 64

Initial Training.. 65

Advanced Training 65

Potential Behavior Problems... 66

Endearing Characteristics 67

Chapter Nine: Decisions and Acquisition 69

Last Minute Reminders.. 71

How to Spot a Healthy Caique 74

Chapter Ten: Conclusion and Summary................................ 77

Your Bird's Home 78

Your Bird's Diet 79

Your Bird's Playtime and Activities................................. 80

Your Bird's Bath and Grooming....................................... 81

Pet Bird Maintenance 82

Potential Problems 82

Glossary of Bird Terms 83

Index.. 89

Photo Credits.. 95

References.. 97

Introduction

A Profile of the Caique Parrot

Caique birds are small sized parrots that are not particularly loud flyers, on their own or as a pair. Not to say that they are utterly silent, because they are in fact vocal little flyers with high shrill calls that have a bit to say. Caiques are hardy little birds that originate from rainforests and live on and feed from tree canopies. In nature you can find these 10-inch tall birds gathering at the top of tree canopies, congregated as they eat and socialize. They are strong little parrots who are active, so if you do decide on getting a caique as a pet make sure that you provide them with a lot of sturdy toys.

These little birds, which originate, eat and breed in South America, lives up on the canopy of trees in the wild, and found primarily in tropical regions of the world. They congregate in small pairs. Other times they can be seen in groups of about 30 birds at the most. They like to gather in pairs and groups in places where there is water. Water is an essential part of living and caique birds are usually found where there is water nearby. In groups, caique birds can be pretty noisy with their bird calls and vocalization.

The caique parrot is an extremely intelligent bird and is likened to the equally smart scarlet macaw in terms of cleverness. The caique parrot is an avid explorer and will check out any new thing it is not familiar with. Leave them outside of their enclosure for a little while and they will surely go for that new little trinket you brought home. They could even go and investigate someone new that they have been introduced to, so make sure that your visitors are given a heads up about your curious caique lest they freak out when they are greeted by your sociable parrot.

These birds can get pretty worked up and react with surprise or become startled when a new situation needs to be dealt with. They can also react pretty strongly to anything out of the ordinary, such as new people in the house, a new purchase (they are the ultimate investigators of all things new, remember?), and even habitual stuff like being set down or placed back into their enclosures.

And since they are very smart birds, it will be important to keep them stimulated both physically and mentally. Caiques do well when they are handled frequently, so make sure that you visit, interact and play with your caique bird often. Doing so will allow the birds get used to you and other handlers in the family.

Caique parrots are not your run-of-the-mill kind of parrots who speak incessantly but they are entertainingly captivating and colourful birds that can be noisy when congregated in numbers. On its own, it is a parrot that makes "tolerable sounds". When buying a caique or adopting one, be sure that you can go and visit the bird before making a commitment. Being given permission to visit the bird will give you an idea of what sort of noises the bird makes and can therefore give you better insight on whether or not the caique would be an acceptable addition to your home without disturbing the neighborhood peace.

Quick Stats on the Caique Parrot

The caique bird is a parrot classified under the Psittacidae family and originates from the shores and regions of South America. There are a two major species of the caique parrot - the black-headed caique and the white-bellied caique; the black-headed caique or the Pionites melanocephala melanocephala is commonly found in Brazil, Roraima, Venezuela and Columbia. Another species of the black-headed caique, the Pionites melanocephala pallida is a native of Peru, Colombia, and Ecuador. One of the white-bellied caique parrot species is known scientifically as the Pionites leucogaster leucogaster, and is found in large numbers between the Amazon and Madeira River basins in Brazil. Another species of the white-bellied caique is the Pionites leucogaster xanthurus, and they are found only in the regions of the Amazonia of Brazil. The Pionites leucogaster xanthomeria is a white-bellied caique bird found in Amazonas regions of Ecuador and Brazil. The size of the colourful caique parrot ranges between 9 to 11 inches with an average size of 10 inches.

The colours of the caique parrot depends on the sort of sub-specie they are. The black-headed caique bird has a black crown, forehead, and nape of the neck. It sports a green streak under its eyes. It has orange-yellow cheeks and its throat is similarly coloured as such. The back wings, the rump and the upper part of the tail of the black-headed caique are green. The breast is colour is cream and this colour trails down all the way to the abdomen of the bird. The black-headed caique has orange-yellow thighs. The legs and beak of the caique parrot is grey in colour and it has orange-coloured irises. The white-bellied caique has an orange crown, forehead and nape. The sides of its head as well as its throat have yellow-coloured feathers. The back wings, the rump and the upper part of the white-bellied caique are green. Its breast and abdomen has a cream-white colouration (giving it its name). The white-bellied caique has green thighs and pink legs. It sports a pale beige bill and has red eyes.

Contrary to popular belief of birds being exclusive eater of seeds, different birds in fact, have different diets. In the wild, and depending on where they come from, caiques have a wide and varied diet that range from fruits from the plants of the awarra, hitia, the acai palm, wild figs, guava and fruits from the warimia tree. The caique would also be seen dining on fruit tree leaves and flowers, like the chewstick, the flowers from the liana plant and the shirada. It also eats the seeds from rubber trees, grumixama, as well as seed heads of rice, American muskwood, the seed from a tamaquare and the mangabe. The caique can also be spotted harvesting nectar and pollen from bacuri plants, the pulp of a chonta palm and the grumixama. Thankfully, commercial bird food is now available and ready for bird owners to feed their pets making it more convenient for an avian pet owner to provide nourishment for their feathered friends.

Caique bird owners now have the option to choose from a variety of bird diets that are made and sold commercially. There are now high quality diet supplement pellets which contain equal quantities of fruits and vegetables. Make sure that you check out the packaging, and most importantly, the ingredients of the bird food you are buying. Be aware that food colouring and food additives to make food more enticing are very bad for the caique parrot. In addition to what is available in the market, a caique bird owner can include a variety of other found-in-nature vegetables and fruits which are also available in grocery stores and supermarkets such as berries, greens, nuts, seeds and legumes. For a "tasty" variety in your caiques diet, toss in a cricket once a week.

You, being the new owner of a caique parrot will need to groom the bird occasionally. Trimming its beak and nails will be something that you will need to make a routine of when you decide to raise caique parrots. Since the caique will be living in close quarters with you, the caique bird will need to be allowed time out of its enclosure for a good stretch; therefore, there will also be the business of clipping its flight feathers a wee bit so that the bird does not accidentally fly out too far or too high.

And because caique parrots are territorial and can display unexpected behaviour when it is surprised or startled, it is best to supervise the initial joining of a caique with other parrots. They are generally protective of their space and get along well with species of their own. There are instances when a caique parrot is integrated with similar-sized parrots that have pleasant dispositions and it has worked. Ultimately, you will want to watch out for any aggression that may cause any of the birds stress. It is best to keep different specie birds from each other unless they are able to coexist peacefully.

In captivity the caique parrot is not as vocal as it would be if it were in the wild. Both of the caique species possess a variety of bird calls, squacks, screeches and shrieks. The black-headed caique parrot, though, makes a tooting sound that is specially its own. It is believed that the black-headed caique does this in order to call out to other caiques. They, just like their cousins, the conures and pionus parrots, possess pretty soft voices, but packs a loud screech. Hence our suggestion of visiting the caique you have your eyes set on before the actual acquisition. These small birds are better able at mimicking environmental sounds than they would human speech and words.

They are bird species who has a long lifespan that can exceed 2 decades and more in captivity. The caique parrot is considered a mature bird between 2 to 3 years. In the wild it finds nesting places in the hollow of tree trunks. They come together and mate toward the tail end of the year, sometime in October, but breeding also largely depends on where the caique is from. Only a DNA test or an endoscopy will be able to determine the sex of the caique parrot. They are constantly chewing on things, so make sure that you provide them with a lot of toys and plenty of replaceable perches.

They are great hoppers, as evidenced by their well-developed and strong legs, and prefer this activity to flying. They are avid bathers, so make sure you have a little bird bath in their enclosure to make them all the happier.

Chapter One: General Description and Distribution

There are two major sorts of caique parrots, and the beauty of these little birds is that they do no differ a lot in terms of personality. Both species and subspecies each possess the playfulness and acrobatic abilities of each other. They are curious explorers who are always on the lookout for the next thing to investigate. They are intelligent little birds who are considered to be the funny guys of the pionus family. They thrive best when they are with their sort, especially in captivity, but could potentially make friends with other like-sized parrots who are tolerant of them as they are of other parrot sorts.

Types of Caique Birds

White - Bellied Caique

The *Pionites leucogaster,* more commonly known as the white-bellied caique call the southern regions of the Amazon, hme. They are found in Northern Brazil to Bolivia. These little birds, which are also seen to congregate in Peru and Ecuador, sport an orange head, their lores, throats and sides of the head the colour of yellow. Its wings and back sport a beautiful green with a creamy-white coloured breast which runs all the way down to its belly. The white-bellied caique has a horn coloured beak, with reddish eyes. When the white-bellied caique is in its juvenile stages, the head looks more brownish with a tuft of black feathers. Its beak sports markings of grey at its base and its eyes are brown. The white bellied caique has two subspecies, one being the one just mentioned. The other sub specie of a white bellied caique can be identified by its green thighs and flanks. Whereas its close cousin, the Yellow - thighed caique has similarly coloured thighs and flanks but has a yellow tail, whereas the white bellied caique has a green tail.

Black - headed caique

The *Pionites melanocephala* or the black-headed caique, sports more of a brownish coloured head which later transforms to black, earning it its name. During the juvenile stages, the black bellied caique sports a belly which looks more yellowish until it turn into the mature cream-white. All the orange and yellow areas of the juvenile black headed caique look paler and only come to full colour upon maturity. Even the band found at the back of the neck is paler in comparison to a much older bird of the same sort. This caique sort is generally in the colour of yellow, having feathers of such on its cheeks, throat, thighs and flanks. An orange band can be found of the hind neck of the specie which is bordered by a few feathers that are a hint of blue. The back wings, rump and upper tail of the black bellied caique are all green. As with its close cousin, the white-bellied caique, the black bellied caique has the similar creamy white coloured belly as its kin. The utmost part of the black bellied caique tail is yellow. It has a grayish black beak with orangey-red eyes.

Determining Caique Parrot Gender

All birds are difficult to sex because their reproductive organs are not visible to the naked eye. Some birds are easier to sex due to distinct male/female colouration. Other times, gender can be determined simply by the size and measure of the bird. But more often than not, sexing a bird is neither an easy nor a comfortable task because it involves invasive probing of its genitalia.

When a juvenile black-headed caique is in its juvenile stage, its head feathers are more of a dark brownish colour with a smattering of black feathers. In essence, if we know which of the caique specie we are looking for, we would be able to tell the sort of caique parrot we are looking at, when we see one, but how about the sex of the parrot? Not so easy to tell with a glance. It is difficult to tell a male from a female bird simply by sight. The only way to test for the bird's gender is to take it to an avian vet to get a DNA test, or via the use of a surgical probe, with a procedure called endoscopy.

Should you be looking to breed your caique parrot, make sure you know what you'll be up for because caique birds can be pretty challenging to breed in captivity for the inexperienced. Given the proper housing, nesting and care that a newly mated female caique will need the proper maintenance and care, the proper bedding and nesting box, caiques could breed successfully. To avoid any major mistakes, it is best that any new caique owner, who intends to breed their birds, consult and work with one who has been recently able to breed them as well.

Lifespan of the Caique Parrot

Caique parrots are hardy little fellas that live long and live well if given the proper care and provided with the right living conditions whilst being raised. Caique parrots in the wild have to contend with big bird predators, and of course, larger opportunistic mammals that are fast enough to capture one of these tiny feathered hoppers. In nature, research has shown that caiques have the ability to live long lives of twenty years and more. Being part of a flock in the wild gives some sort of assurance and safety to the caique parrots because there is always usually one or two caique parrots who act as look out for the other caiques in the flock, which are up in the canopy, when it is feeding time. The beauty of caiques is that they like to congregate in small groups of about 8-10 birds, essentially part of a posse that gives them safety in numbers.

In captivity, there have been caique parrots that have been reported to live for more than over 2 decades! Providing the proper living facilities, giving the caique parrots the essential nutrition they require and ample socialization time ensures the long life of your caique parrots. With proper cage maintenance, which includes enclosure upkeep and cleaning, changing the bird bath and water bowl, replacing base-cage sheets, are some of the ways you can ensure a clean lifestyle for your messy buddy. Not having the social graces at the table, caiques are much like their other feathered cousins when it comes to eating , drinking and playing - they can make a pretty good job of soiling up the stuff that is inside of their cages. To allow your caique bird the longevity it is actually afforded, maintaining daily cleanliness and routine sanitation the of bird abode is crucial.

Chapter Two: Choosing a Caique Parrot

In this section we shall be discussing the procedures on how to acquire, whether by purchase or adoption, a caique bird. Now it has to be said that caique parrots are indeed amusing birds that have a tendency to vocalize a little bit. We say "a little bit" because, a caique, like the pionus parrot, is not the best at vocalizing human words, but they do make bird sounds and calls. When alone or as a pair, the caique birds call is tolerable and in fact, pretty relaxing. The discussion takes a turn if we start talking about a flock of them; they can get pretty loud when they are congregated together. Therefore, it is but wise to pay caique birds that are being given up for adoption, or those that are for purchase, a visit.

This way, you will have an idea of how much sounds they make and if this is something that is within the tolerance of yourself and of course, your neighbors. In the wild caique parrots stay atop the canopy of the trees where they favour to frolic, play, exercise, forage and eat. When in the care of a pet owner, the caique will require you to provide everything it would need in order for the bird to thrive well. It is important that you get a healthy caique bird. Not determining its origin, history and health could spell disastrous for your bird and a pile of medical bills on your end.

When looking for a caique parrot, doing your bit to investigate the best candidates will set you and the parrot up for a successful union. Not taking the time and choosing the first one that you see could mean problematic days ahead. Since caique birds are known to live a pretty long lifespan - up to 20 years and even more! - it is best to scout out these playful little birds from aviary adoption centers or shelters, or owners who might have more than they had bargained for. The beauty about adoption is that, the birds would've normally gotten the proper exposure to people and have been socialized to a certain extent, making them more open to the presence of humans. But do beware that caique birds are loyal little flyers and will be a little skittish or aloof at the onset of the meeting.

Adopting a Caique

When adopting a caique bird, make sure that you are given amply moderate access to the bird before the actual turnover, that way the bird is not freaked out by your presence which makes for a better transition period when you bring home your new caque buddies. This will give you and the birds the proper amount of time to get to use to each other. Transporting caique birds could take a bit of toll on the bird, so be careful that you have the proper equipment - a transporting cage with a cover - for road or air travel.

Assuming that everything went good during your visits, the next thing to do is prepare for their move to your place by having set up their space and enclosures - with all the fittings and furnishings - before the actual transfer of the caiques to your home. By this time, you would have been stocked up on the proper bird food to give them a welcome feast after what could be an arduous experience for them. Should the birds react, and act a little displaced at the start, fret not. If you give them just enough time, they will get used to their new digs and, you, their new human friend.

Bird Sanctuaries

With more and more parrot sanctuaries mushrooming around the country, it is apparent that many have perhaps bitten off more than they can chew with their pet birds. Other reasons for caiques finding its way to avian sanctuaries abounds; divorce, death, a residential move, a job transfer, etc. Many of these people perhaps did not have a choice in leaving their feathery buddies behind, and they are just waiting for someone like you to come, rescue, and keep them. Think long and hard about how you want to acquire a pet bird and if possible make your first option one of adoption. Not only would you be saving a ton of money in terms of purchasing a bird that has never been owned before. You get the perks of joining up with a caique that has been housebroken, socialized and trained to mingle with people.

Caique Breeders

Acquiring a caique parrot from a breeder would be another avenue you could take in terms of procurement of said bird. Finding a reputable breeder in your area is almost heaven sent as caique bird owners are scattered throughout the country. The convenience of purchasing from a breeder is that you should be provided with a guarantee in case of anything happening later on after you take home your birds. A guarantee would almost usually include preliminary and initial medical checkups and vaccination given to bird. The birds would have gotten the proper care and would have been exposed to the correct socialization it would need in order to thrive and live amongst humans.

Health of the Caique

It is important that you know of the history of the birds you are acquiring, unless you are comfortable with surprises, have deep pockets and your aim is really to help out a caique in need at all costs. Since the caique bird naturally lives a pretty long life, you may later on want to give it company. It's important that birds are checked out extensively by a certified avian vet.

Chapter Three: Maintaining Wellness of the Caique Bird

Knowing what caique birds would need is an important bit you need to determine early on in order for your caique bird to have a good environment wherein it can thrive and grow well. You will hear about the relation of health and wellbeing of pets to clean enclosures and this is something we cannot stress enough. Any person who intends to take in a new pet, any sort of pet, is expected to learn about the health and condition of the animal they plan on taking in and raising it.

Doing so not only assures you of a healthy pet whose company you will get to enjoy for years to come, this will also secure your financial expenses to a minimum as you do the right things to keeping your bird healthy.

Proper food and feeding schedules

Knowing what to feed your caique birds is an important bit to understand if you want your parrots to thrive well both physically and mentally. All parrot species, big or small, have certain preferences for the food they seek out in the wild. Whilst some parrots like the Macau, prefer to dine on seeds, other parrots like the pionus, love the taste of nectar. The caique parrot is no different when prefering some food sorts over others. The caique birds, for some reason, gravitate toward colourful flowers in the wild. They also seem to go for sweet tasting fruits they find in nature. A new caique pet owner should take the time to spend with their birds in order to determine the caique bird's preference for food. Of course, you must be initially aware of the foods they do zero in on to determine this.

In captivity, caique owners have observed that their caique birds prefer fruits such as grapes, pomegranates, apples, papaya, dried figs, cranberries, blueberries, apples, oranges, dried figs, etc. They also seem to favour corn, carrots, broccoli, green beans, snap peas, etc.

Cutting up their food in small portions big enough for their feet to pick up is the easiest way to entice a bird to eat their food. Not that they would need any coaxing from you, if the food you provide them are the ones they prefer and are nourished by correctly.

They may also be fed bird pellet food that can be found in the pet trade market. There are formulated diets that can be bought in pet shops and supermarkets that contain the proper amount of supplemental nutrition that is good for the caique birds you own. Be sure that you give them the proper ratio and portions of varied foods. You want to give them a feeding ratio of 45% formulated pellets: 35% fruits and veggies: 20% bird seed. Avoid giving caique birds too much bird seed because too much of bird seed can cause them to develop increased lipid levels in their blood supply which can cause their feathers to change colours out of their usual hues.

Serve up a bowl of the fresh foods you have diligently cut up for them, in the day time, allowing the birds to gobble up bits of food throughout the day. Experience has proven that scattering about a tablespoon full of sunflower seeds on the floor of their cage gives them a nice light snack after you have removed their fresh food bowl in the evening. If you are looking to breed your caiques then an important addition to their food fare would be protein, especially during the late autumn, early winter mating season.

Breeding avians also require essential minerals, particularly calcium, which helps strengthen the eggshells of the clutch. You will notice that before the caique hen lays its eggs, she will noticeably become obsessed on chewing on anything that has minerals in it. You can supply your laden caique hen with a fresh cuttlebone. You may also want to add an oyster shell that would do the job as well. In addition, you can also provide them with a meant-for-human calcium tablet.

Without overdoing it, share a small piece of meat from your plate that has not been doused in artificial whatnots and that should hit the spot. They also like the occasional soft bodied larvae, and need essential amino acids that can only come from animal sourced meats. Manufacturers of formulated pellets include these in the pellets they make, but you can switch it up and serve up a half-inch slice of yellow cheese. Give them treats like the occasional pecan or walnut and of course, sunflower seeds can also be used as treats. Another treat they seem to like, whether in the wild or in captivity, is nectar. The caique bird, in nature, would gravitate toward the bacuri tree which produced a cup-like blossom which contains the sweet nectar they oh-so love. The caique bird is an integral part of the natural life of nature since it acts as a pollinator of flora. Always remember to freshen up thei bird and drinking bowls with clean water. Providing them with clean water at all times ensures that water they drink or bathe in is not contaminated or murky.

Maintenance of enclosure

Avian vets do not come cheap nor are there too many of them, so seek out one long before you start the process of acquiring your birds and their equipment. Make sure that your avian vet is not transiting or moving anytime soon, and that they can be reached and consulted for any eventualities in the future. The reason we mention this, is because, avian vets have determined that most diseases suffered by a bird is due to unkempt and unsanitary cage conditions. Make sure that you give the cage of the birds, daily maintenance by clearing out soiled floor lining (you may use newspapers for this task). Make it a point that bird baths and drinking bowls are replaced with fresh clean water regularly. Some people like to do it once in the morning, and again at night. However, should the water immediately become murky with food debris or bird poop, make sure that it is replaced immediately.

Maintenance of enclosure mean taking stock of not only the cleanliness of the cage, it also includes all the fittings and furnishings you have placed inside of the cage. It will be important for you to realize that investing on the best sundries that will last you and your birds.

You want to avoid using any furnishings that have toxic ingredients in them. Ceramic or stainless steel bowls are the best and most durable of drinking, feeding and bird bath bowls. You will also need to remove and replace swings, perches and twigs that are inside of the cage when they have deteriorated or when they are too banged up for proper utilization.

Chapter Four: Required Space, Enclosure and Sundries

The colourful and hardly vocal Caique parrot is indeed a small bird in comparison to other medium sized parrots. However, they will utilize every square inch of the cage you provide for them. Again, the size of your active caique bird, which will be no more than 10 inches from head to claw, and how many you decide to commit to, will determine the space you will need for the proper enclosure they will need.

Housing Requirements

For an individual or a couple living in a small spaced apartment and is looking to get a caique parrot, you will be glad to know that a 24x24x18 will be sufficient and ample space to provide your caique bird. Make sure though that you remember to keep windows and doors closed when you have trained your bird well enough and it is allowed to fly and roam freely around a controlled space.

Get to know the Caique parrot in this chapter and find out all about the little guys with their colourful feathers and how to best showcase and enjoy them. A truly great companion and well able to survive and thrive solo, the caique is a parrot that is fairly independent and can amuse itself during times of the day when you are out of the house. Be sure though, that you not only provide it with toys to keep it occupied but remember to set aside ample play time with your caique.

In order for birds, like the caique parrot, to live to its fullest potential and enjoy a life in the safety of captivity, you as its new caregiver will need to provide it with. Make sure that you have enough space in your home to house a caique bird comfortably. Caique birds are pretty quiet birds save for the occasional tweeting and chirping since they are not big talkers, so they will be perfect pets for those living in close proximity to their neighbors.

Bird Housing, Toys, Playpens and other Equipment

The size of the cage you should get will depend on the number of caique birds you intend to raise. The more the birds, the bigger the cage needed to house them all. Of course, you will have to add more cages later on if you intend to breed the caique birds under your wing. You will also need a smaller spare cage for quarantine purposes - this will be used for any new birds you will be bringing into the brood. New birds that come into your care should be quarantined and removed from the general population to avoid any transference of illness. Nesting boxes will also be needed for caiques that will be paired off for mating and breeding.

Your caique parrots are active and playful birds so they will need all the toys they can get their little feet on. Choose toys that will allow them the proper sort of exercise whilst inside their enclosures. They will need perches and swings, and twigs and things that will not only get them moving but also ones that will engage their inquisitive minds. They will need the right amount of air space in their enclosure where they can flit and fly.

They are not big flyers, in the wild or otherwise, but they are pretty dexterous hoppers, so make it a point that they have a lot of floor space to show off their skills. In addition to the sundries mentioned previously, you will also want to furnish the cage with chains and bells - they like shiny objects they can push around and play with. Hang a few climbing ropes at the opposite side of the swing you fit the cage with, and marvel at the dexterity of your caique parrot. Add in a small wooden bird cage inside of its enclosure where the birds can retreat to when they want some peace and quiet.

Housing and Bird Cages:

The size of a standard cage that will fit a caique parrot comfortably is a cage with dimensions of 40"-50" high with a floor space of about 24" x 40". But of course, if you can afford the space in your home, a bigger cage would be a lot better. Ideally you want to purchase a stainless steel cage, which would last longer, with specs of 24"x 24" x 32"with the bar spacing under an inch wide, preferably ¾ of an inch apart. The best rule of thumb is to invest on a sturdy enclosure that provides a lot of room for movement and ample space for all the sundries, furnishings, feeding and drinking dishes, bird bath and playthings that will be needed by your caique birds. These cages should be roomy enough and not make the bird feel constricted in movement. As long as the room is kept warm enough for the birds, they will be fine. Caique birds do not need specialized temperatures; however, one of the most important fixtures they will need would be proper lighting in their enclosure

Aviary

Should you be fortunate enough to be living in a region where the climate is temperate and conducive to caique birds, and if you have a lot of outside space, then you might want to consider building an aviary for your caique birds.

Chapter Five: Breeding a Caique Parrot

Breeding caiques can take more than a while to achieve. Breeding them takes study, research, patience, and, without causing harm to the birds, experimentation with nesting and bedding techniques. In the wild caique parrots would normally be able to find everything they would need in order to nest and brood their eggs. The dynamics change dramatically when the caiques that are breeding are bred in captivity. It is best to apprentice with or collaborate with an experienced and recently successful caique bird breeder.

Breeding Basics

If you are planning on getting a mating pair, a male and female that is, it is best that you get them from one place where they have initially been seen to bond. It takes at least two years for a caique parrot to mature and only then can they start mating. A breeder of birds would usually have the information on the bird's gender through DNA testing or an endoscopy. However, carrying out these procedures too early on could result in a false identification of gender. It is best to wait to sex the birds until such time they reach near maturity.

Possibly the most challenging aspect of breeding caiques would be finding the right mating pair. Caiques are choosy when it comes to the partners they pick. They don't like being forced on one another and prefers to take their own time when singling out their match. Be aware that black-headed caiques in particular can become agitated when forced to mate with another one of their sort. In order to increase the chances of birds finding their mates, procure at least 4-5 birds of each gender. Make provisions for small separate cages which you want to set side by side. You want to observe how they relate and get along, or otherwise, with each other. When you observe a pair gravitate toward each other, you may have found your pair!

You can then proceed to place both of the birds in a bigger enclosure. Make sure that you do this at a time when you are free to observe and supervise the initial union, throughout the following days. If this pairing goes of without aggression or fighting, then you should be fine. Allow the birds to settle in and get to know each other in close quarters. It may take them a bit of time to get used to their new mate.

Pay mind when you buy pairs that breed. Make sure that you get all the details of the birds including and importantly, the history of the hen. Determine that the hen has no history of devouring its eggs after it has laid them. To be on the safe side, when it comes to breeding caiques, it is best to look for birds that are at least 3 years old. Not only would they be mature enough to mate, they would also have been exposed and socialized to mingling with other birds. Although caiques are able to breed at 2 years of age, they may not be mature enough to nest and they could potentially destroy their hatchlings.

Determine the health and wellness of the birds as these birds. Make sure that the birds are not closely related and that they are of good health. Have the birds checked with your own avian vet once you take them home. It is advised that the birds be quarantined and kept from any other birds you may have in order to decrease the chances of a sick bird passing on an illness to a healthy bird.

A caique will not need too much space to nest after a successful mating. Provide for them a small cage with dimensions of 24 high x 24 wide x 48 long. MAke sure that the cage is reinforced and that no big animals r rodents can get to the birds during nesting. A successful breeding pair would yield at least 2 clutches a year. Do not be surprised if they yield more than this in a year, because this is a possibility. If you are not looking to breed more than what you are ready for, make sure that you separate the pair.

Things you want to keep in mind before the breeding season starts

- Make sure that the birds' sexes have been determined to avoid frustration and wasted time. DNA sexing is the best way to determine the gender of your caique birds and even that can yield false identification. To ensure that you are getting the correct gender information of the bird, wait until the bird is about 2-3 years into maturity before carrying out the test.

- Place the intended pair in separate cages that is about an inch away from each other. You will then have to observe how they interact with each other. Are they cautiously curious? Do they seem to be checking each other out without aggression? Or do they seem weary and suspicious of each other? If they are showing no inclination or even hostility to each other, you will have to repeat the process of choosing another mate. If they are interacting well with each other then follow the next step;

- Since all birds, especially the caique parrot, are teritorial, it is best to place them in a cage that has not been used before. A new cage will be their neutral ground, where teritory has not been established, therefore giving them freer reign of exploring the new enclosure together - an ultimately, each other.

- If there is no other cage to spare, then it is best that the hen is placed in the breeding box with the male being introduced later to the enclosure. Once they are in one enclosure, keep an eye out on the two of them for the next two weeks or so. Spats and squabbles are normal behaviors that caique birds display. What you want to see the birds achieve is them sitting with each other and preening each other as well. These are common signs of the birds pairing off well.

Breeding and Breeding Environment

Make sure that the facilities provided for the caique birds you take in are suitable facilities that would induce proper mating and nesting. Given the proper lighting, heating and environmental conditions, caique birds can in fact mate all year round. Caique parrots are not difficult to breed given the proper, conducive environment the pair of birds would need for a successful mating. The mating caique pair would not only need cages where they can get to know and be around each other during mating season, they would also need a suitably sized, properly furnished nesting box. Caique parrots that are kept indoors can breed all year round and a productive, breeding pair can yield multiple clutches. This of course, largely depends on how soon after the babies leave the nest.

Cages of 24 x 24 x 18, one that is made of rust-proof stainless steel would be the suitable enclosure as other cages have the tendency to rust and corrode. Your caique birds are some of the most inquisitive sorts of parrots and if they get too curious about the rust build up, they may start chipping away at this, and unknowingly ingest toxic paint chips, corroded metals and bits of the cage debris. Be sure to set them up in a proper cage that would not deteriorate so easily or wear out too soon.

Make an investment on the enclosures of your birds as this is something they will be using for a long time to come.

Egg Laying and Hatchlings:

A caique parrot hen will look heavy and swollen in its vent region just shortly before it lays its eggs. You can also tell that a caique hen is ready to lay her clutch when you see massive droppings. The average number of eggs a caique hen would be anywhere from three to four eggs at a time. However, do not be surprised if you find five or six eggs, because that is a probability, the female caique parrot will typically lay an egg every three days until the female has laid the whole lot. Caique hens will It could take a couple of tries for a new breeding pair to get a proper clutch lain, so it is also important for you to know that there would be possibilities of the caique hen to push out transparent eggs before actual fertile eggs are produced and chicks are hatched.

Be aware and know that if a mating pair is inexperienced, they may ultimately damage and destroy their own eggs or even their chicks. An instance that may bring about this destructive behaviour toward their offspring could be a squabble between the mating pair that may cause destruction to the laid egg.

When an egg has been damaged, the caique birds may eat the the damaged egg to keep the nesting box clean. Should you notice the caique birds deliberately destroying their yield of eggs, you want to pull a quick switch-a-roo and replace the real egg with a wooden or ceramic egg. The destructive parental pair, once they realize that the eggs can't be destroyed will eventually settle down and do the needful. However, if the destruction of eggs continues, you will have to do some investigative work to figure out which of the two is the culprit. Should you determine the male caique to be the destroyer, you will have to remove it from the cage, the night before the next egg is laid.

Once the hen lays the next egg, be sure to retrieve the egg and replace it with the ceramic or wooden "dummy-egg". There is little you can do but attempt to retrieve a newly laid egg, if you discover the caique hen to be the culprit of the destruction. If it is indeed the female caique causing the egg breakage, then make sure that you are on-hand to watch out for the next egg to be laid and replace it immediately with a dummy-egg.

Should the mating pair of caique parrots be the rowdy sort, then, make sure that you remove and replace the real eggs with the ceramic dummy eggs. Move the newly laid eggs to another enclosure where a nesting pair of caique birds can foster the eggs removed from the rowdy pair's box. Replace the eggs you removed with transparent or infertile eggs that another pair produced.

The reasoning for this is that you will need to determine who the source of the destruction of eggs is. Again, an inexperienced pair can destroy their clutch a few times before they settle down and start nesting correctly.

Incubation

The period of incubation for caique birds is around twenty to twenty five days. There are some caique hens that will stay put and sit tight shortly after laying the initial egg. There can be a wide margin between the oldest and youngest chicks especially in a large clutch. It is important that you have been apprenticing with an experienced caique breeder in order to know what to expect when expecting. With the proper equipment, which is a candling light, a trained eye can usually observe the eggs fertility five days after the incubation period starts. The caique hen will only exit the nesting box to defecate and would spend most of her time tending to incubate her eggs. The male caique plays quite the role of the expectant father during this period, helping nourish its partner by feeding her through the nesting box hole. It is not unusual for the male to take their turn in incubating the eggs, and can be quite a sight to see; another endearing characteristic of the caique bird.

Breeding Caique Parrot Laws in the United States

The rise of bird population in avian sanctuaries and the mushrooming of these sanctuaries is evidence of people giving up birds due to uninformed decisions and misinformation about the health and, more importantly, the care of these birds. This is why it is it is important that anyone intending to acquire and raise a pet, understand that there are responsibilities that trail after taking care of any animal. It is also vital that the pet you decide to take in is not an animal that is listed as endangered or near endangerment.

More and more parrot's species are coming dangerously close to being endangered. With illegal poaching so prevalent and eager to make a quick buck, the problem of illegal captures of animals in the wild has become more and more of a concern to conservationist. Recently, even parrot species who are not endangered of extinction, has been given protection by local and international animal welfare agencies, like the Convention on International Trade in Endangered Species of Wild Fauna and Flora or CITES, to avert the possible wiping out of these parrots species.

Any potential buyer and would-be parrot carer will have to abide to a set of rules and follow regulations in order to stave off the increased illegal capture of close to endangered and endangered parrot's species from entering the pet trade market of the US. Purchasing parrots is not illegal, but there are rules to be observed as to how these birds are obtained, how they are transported, the papers a potential owner would need to justify the proper collection of the bird, etc.

Determine the national laws of your home country and figure out what they state about purchasing, shipping, raising and breeding of parrots. Familiarize yourself with existing regulations to avoid any problems that may arise later on. Owning and breeding parrots are different from one country to the next, so do not assume anything. Be proactive and determine the truth.

It is advised that parrot owners and breeders provide their breeding birds with individual identification. Identifiable markings, like leg-bands and tattoos are a common practice to give identification to the bird; in the event it gets lost or if it flies out the window, doing so will also be convenient for the continued update of the genealogical and medical documents of the bird.

Upstanding breeders of birds and parrots provide their young birds an identifying leg band. Closed leg bands are ideal to determine identification of a lost bird.

Alternatively, implanted microchips under the bird's skin or muscle is also one other reliable and less obvious means to identify the bird. It may be an uncomfortable procedure at first (more for the bird than you) but it will serve the bird and you better in the long run. Aside from the two previous options, a bird can also be given a tattoo marking as a form of identifying the bird. However, be aware that the tattoo can (and probably will) fade over time. Bird footprints are also used as a tool to identify birds.

There are no laws against purchasing, owning or breeding caique birds in the United States and caique birds are thankfully not listed as an endangered species in any of the animal welfare agencies around the world. But it is still your responsibility to figure these details out before making the jump on purchasing and raising a caique parrot.

Chapter Six: Kids and Parrots

We've seen it time and again, kids seeing talking parrots in movies and immediately wanting one for themselves. How does one deal with this situation? If you have recently found yourself in this situation - a tug of war of sorts with your offspring - on whether or not to get a caiaque, then have we got information for you that you will want to read. Getting a parrot entails work and responsibilities. Slacking off is just not acceptable when choosing parrots as pets, or you will otherwise end up with a mess of a house that will smell. As much as they are easy to take care of, there are specific methods one would need to follow, and have become second nature, in order for the bird to thrive and thrive well. Setting clear expectations is just the smartest thing you can do.

Reminders When Keeping Parrots

First off, we need to remember that taking in any animal has their drawbacks and risks. Parrots are no different. Whether large or small, parrots are ultimately animals of the wild and even the tamest parrot can inflict unintentional injury to people. In the wild they use their claws and beaks as a defense mechanism to ward of injury to self or possible, impending predation. In captivity, injury, accidental or otherwise, can occur if a bird is handled roughly, when it is startled or if it itself gets hurt or attacked. Children are in particular risk of these unintended attacks because children can get pretty excited. Their quick movements, loud and sudden shrieks and noises can often becoming alarming to birds and may disrupt their peace. Be mindful that all visits between parrot and child are supervised by a responsible adult who would know how to deter an event that could cause injury to either child or bird.

Parrots are known to live for a very long time in nature. In captivity, when well taken care of, a parrot can live up to and beyond 20 years. That is a pretty amazing feat of existence! If you are not the sort who is willing to commit to the responsibilities of a pet owner, then, it is not proper for the child to be given one.

However, if you are an individual looking to get a pet companion for the long haul, then a caique parrot just may be the pet for you. A caique parrot is not hard to raise as long as its specific needs are met. Under the correct conditions, given the proper care and attention, a caique parrot is known to live for many decades, so make sure that you are aware of the implications and responsibilities of taking on a caique bird would be to your lifestyle and way of life.

Does your present home have enough space to fit in a birdhouse? A caique may be small but it will need a lot of air space to fly around in and, being the clown it is, it will need enough floor area and hopping space for its clowning around and comic antics. The lack of space will be difficult to contend with if the bird is not given enough space to move. This may cause the bird stress and which could lead to worse medical conditions that would equate to medical and doctor bills. Since they do live a pretty long time, you will have to consider the long haul on food supplies. Depending on how many caiques you decide you can afford to raise, you will need to crunch the numbers of how much it will cost to feed them, along with yourself, and possibly even the family. In short, you will have to factor in monthly spending on the birds annual needs such as its monthly food, daily vitamins, and sundries like toys or exercise equipment.

Then you will also need to factor in annual visits to an avian vet. An avian vet is a specialty; therefore, their fees do not come cheap. Since a child does not earn a living, it will largely be on you to get expenses sorted out. You will have to be thoughtful about taking on any sort of pet, because as you may have already noticed, the responsibility of a pet will largely fall on the one who understands the weight of raising something with life.

Parrots can be a lot of work. For something so small - a lot smaller than your tiny child - they can also take up quite a bit of space. Birds are naturally messy eaters, and drinkers, making jobs of cleaning up a little more routine since cleaning does need to be done on a daily basis. A kept cage is a healthy cage. Most bird ailments stem from unkempt cages and soiled food and water. Should your little tyke be asking for a parrot, its best that you sit them down and talk to them about the responsibilities of cleaning up after the birds, as well as feeding and hydrating the little flyers.

Parrots need large enclosures where they can fly and hop about in and these cages will surely get its share of grime and dirt on an everyday occurrence. Making sure that your child is old enough to take on some of the responsibilities will not only mold the child to proper and responsible pet care, they would also be made aware of the job which entails being owner of a pet. If your child is not old enough to take care of one part of the time, then make sure that you are willing to pick up the slack. The decision on whether the child is ready for the responsibility of owning a pet will fall on you. You taking the time out today to research on the caique parrot, whether for your child or yourself, are a truly good way to start off your journey taking in a caique bird

Chapter Seven: Hygiene and Nutrition of the Caique Parrot

As with any other pet, whether it be of the terrestrial or avian sort, pets need to eat - and eat the proper food. So knowing what to feed them is an important bit of information that all potential pet owners should know. This also goes for your avian pet. Each parrot species has specific foods they eat which are available in their original habitat and they have access to these by the grace of Nature. By now, you are well aware, that in captivity, you as their new caregiver will have to take on the responsibility of looking for their sustenance and feeding your birds.

All parrots have different taste in food fare and have varied nutritional needs. The nutritional value of one parrot does not apply to another. Whilst some parrots like seeds, and other prefer nectar, caiques in the wild would not pass up a colourfully bright flower.

Caring for and Feeding Your Caique Parrot:

Knowing what to provide your pets in terms of sustenance is an important aspect of them enjoying good health. Ill-nourished birds would show lethargy, moodiness, and possibly distress, if not provided with elements and sustenance that would closely resemble what life would be like in the wild, minus the predation. A properly-nourished caique equates to it living up to its full potential with a happy disposition to boot. Keep in mind that the conditions of its cage will play a large hand on its good health, so make it a routine to keep your caique cage clean. CHange up any newspaper base covers on a regular basis, once a day at the very least. Importantly, do not forget to replace their bath and drinking bowls with fresh water twice a day. As earlier discussed, birds are can get pretty "clumsy" when feeding, so food remnants could fester in their drinking bowls and could be cause for upset stomachs, or worse, intestinal bacteria.

Bird Food and Formulated Diet

Make sure that you are providing the sort of food the caiques require in order for them to stay healthy and strong. Caiques love sweet tasting food, so make sure that you provide their favourite fruits and vegetables so that they get the proper nourishment for their little legs, bodies and minds to operate to their optimum best. Formulated pellets manufactured by bird pellet makers, contain the proper amount of nutrients the birds would need, but you will want to give your caique birds a variety of foods so they don't get bored with the food served up to the, Make sure that you give them a proper ratio of pellets, and fresh fruits and vegetables each day. Give them occasional treats like, nuts and soft bodied larvae.

You may offer them the infrequent it of meat, that would provide them with much needed amino acids. Set out for them their feeding bowls in the daytime with enough food that they can pick and feed on throughout the day whilst you are out and remember to remove unfinished food by evening. You can scatter a tablespoon full of sunflower seeds that the birds can snack on during the night time. Commercially formulated pellet diets are created in a way that it provides the complete nutritional needs of a caique parrot. However, you want to give your caique birds a variety of fresh foods that will keep them looking forward to meal times.

Seed Diet

Keep seed diets at a low 20% of their total daily intake. Too much of seeds can be bad for the birds, and they can be consumed by contending with the seeds that they lose interest in the fresh food bowls you lay out for them. Give seeds as treats instead to fulfill this dietary need of the birds. Never feed the birds a diet of bird seed alone as these birds have a wide variety of available foods that are available to them in the wild and that they have access to as well.

Grooming Your Caique Parrots

For a new caique bird owner to live up to their responsibilities toward their new feathered buddies, they would need to pay mind to grooming their birds. Bird grooming is not only beneficial for the captive caique parrots complete wellness, grooming time also give both you and the birds to spend time with each other. Routine grooming will also allow you, its responsible caregiver, to notice any anomalies or abnormalities that are otherwise not apparent to the naked eye. The caique parrot is a lovable bird who loves being doted on by its favourite humans. They find pleasure in spending time with you, therefore grooming, if done correctly - sans injury to bird - will strengthen the bond between bird and human.

Bird Baths

Caique parrots much like their close feathered parrot kin, adore a refreshing rain shower. They have been observed to continue with frolic and play under a light rain shower. The secret to raising happy, healthy birds is not really a secret at all, but you should be aware that in order for your caique birds to thrive well, you will need to closely replicate what their natural environment would provide. This would include spraying or lightly misting them on a weekly basis. Keep a misting bottle that will be used exclusively to mist your birds. Do not reuse misters that have been used to contain chemicals as this will harm your bird. Purchase a mister that will be used exclusively for the birds. Another option would be to set up a shower sprayer that would lightly mist the general bird population of the enclosure. Make sure that after misting this way, that you replace all base - sheeting that cover the floor of the cage.

Wings

Clipping the wings of a juvenile bird who has not learnt how to use them in flight is ill-advised. Do not do this until the bird has comfortably been able to understand the work of its wings. However, once they are big enough, you will need to take your birds to an expert groomer or an avian vet to carry out this task. Do not attempt to clip the wings of your bird on your own via a YouTube tutorial. It is best to learn how to clip your birds' wings by repeatedly observing an experienced individual do it. Not clipping your mature caique parrot's wings may ultimately result in them escaping through an open window or door. Over clipping a bird's wings could also result in bird accidents and crashes, which may result in bird injury. This is a good time remind and encourage new caique bird owners and potential caique caregivers, to network and collaborate with experienced caique bird owners.

Beak

There are ways for the bird to keep their beak size in check. Provide it with items that will help them perform a natural habit of trimming down their beaks. You will be able to find these items available at pet/bird shops, like mineral blocks and lava blocks that help them keep their beak size in check. With enough instruction and demonstration from an experienced bird groomer or avian vet, you can help them file down their beaks with the use of an emery board. Again it is not advised that you do this without an expert present.

Nails

The claws and nails of your parrot serves a purpose but having them overgrow to abnormal proportions will inhibit the natural movements and antics your caique bird likes so much. Overgrown nails prevent the birds from hopping and perching properly. When nails are overgrown and left to grow, the birds may ultimately injure you during socialization, play and handling. There are items to keep their nail growth in check, which they can utilize on their own, if available in their enclosure. Choose perches that will help keep their nails in check.

Should this not be enough, you can employ a pair of clipper to trim its nails down. Be sure though that you have had proper instructions and have witnessed enough nail clipping procedures before carrying out the task on your own. Much like clipping a dog or cat's nails, cliping the nails of a bird has to be precise. Cutting too far into the quick of the nail will result in profuse bleeding. If it happens, make sure that you have a small mound of flour that you can dip your injured caique toe in.

Chapter Eight: Bird Proofing Rooms and Training Your Caique

When you have a bird for a pet, you need to make sure that not only its cage is safe and secure but also it's surrounding environment. There are many domestic hazards that can be dangerous to your Caique, physically and even psychologically. Some threats may bring mild reactions, while others may result in instant death. It is important to bird-proof your home to keep your pet Caique healthy and protected.

Bird Proofing Your House

- As with any other pet, never leave a child and your pet bird unsupervised especially active, over-excited Caiques. While they are good pets, children—even adults—who don't know how to handle them can hurt the bird or get hurt themselves. Make it a point to teach your children how to care for and handle your Caique in a safe manner. This is applicable for any kind of pet you have in your home.

- If you have an aquarium, it is best to cover it so that your Caique will not accidentally ingest a fish or drown in it. If you have other pets such as dogs, cats or reptiles, make sure that their cages are placed in different areas of the house so they don't harm each other.

- The cage is your bird's home; make sure that it is placed in a safe and comfortable place. Avoid locations that are too hot, too drafty or too cold. You can put a blanket cover on your cage at night to add extra security to your pet. Do not place your cage near any kind of fan as your bird may accidentally be sucked into it when it is out of the cage. Do not place it near heating lamps or things that have cords.

- When bringing your bird out of the cage for play time and exercise, make sure that all windows are closed, shut and covered. Birds are not familiar with glass panes and when uncovered, our bird might slam into them.

- When you cover your glass windows or panes, you are preventing your bird from seeing the outdoors and will keep it interested on what is inside the house.

- Make sure that the screens on your windows are mounted securely and that there are no holes wherein your pet bird can get trapped or injured. As a precaution, you might want to clip your Caique's wings to slow down its flight. You can also place a lanyard on one of its legs to limit its flight span. Trim your bird's nails regularly to that they don't snag drapes, curtains and table cloths which can lead to injury.

- Keep your bird away from cluttered rooms as well as rooms with breakables, electronic equipment and mechanical devices. Your bird may get injured or trapped in wires, broken glass and the likes.

- Caiques are inquisitive, energetic birds that like to get into small spaces. Make sure they are not hiding in cupboards or cabinets before you close such. Also avoid bringing them near corners and nooks lest they think it's a good place to nest and you won't be able to find them.

- Cover all air ducts so your bird won't crawl into them and get lost or injured.

- Tinsel and Christmas decorations, like cords and wires, can entrap your birds and injure them accidentally. Make sure you keep your bird away from these when playing outside its cage.

- Before you throw in your laundry into the washer or dryer, or when you lay new bed sheets, check that your bird is safe in its cage because you may not notice it walking into sheets or clothes and accidentally hurt them.

- When you are cooking, make sure that your bird is safe in its cage. Open pots, steam, fumes and even chemical solutions pose a threat to your Caique. Even the simple butter or margarine can cause your Caique's feathers to be matted and render it immobile.

- Remember that not all human food is okay for your pet bird. Avocados, salt, coffee beans, tea, onion, garlic, yeast dough and caffeinated beverages can cause illness or death when ingested.

- Keep your toilet and bathroom doors closed. Not only will accidentally inhaled fumes cause death to your bird, they might also drown in water reservoirs.

- When you use chemical solutions for cleaning your home, make sure that your bird is safe in its cage so that they won't inhale fumes or accidentally drink toxic chemicals.

- Never use herbicides, insecticides and pesticides near your bird.

- Make sure that the cage is free from zinc, arsenic and lead as these chemicals are dangerous to your Caique, as with other animals.

Training and Handling Caique Parrots

When you get a Caique, you need to understand that you have a very intelligent bird. It will be easy to teach them tricks and they will enjoy learning them. Caiques are most likely to show off what they know. However, they are strong-willed birds and you need to be firm when you are handling them—they need to know who the boss is. If you are the one who is tame during your training, they will establish dominance and never follow you. Caiques are not the kinds of pets for beginners. They will only frustrate their new owners. However, when they are raised correctly, Caiques are the best companions anyone can have.

Taming Basics

Slow and steady always does the trick when it comes to handling and training a Caique. Like any other pet, you should let it grow accustomed to your voice, your presence and its new environment when it arrives home. Give it a few days to be comfortable and to trust you before you start taming and handling it. If you get a handfed baby Caique, you won't have much trouble handling it as it is already used to human care. Most parrots are receptive to evening training and Caiques are no different.

Make sure that you limit your sessions to less than 20 minutes and have an hour's rest before you begin a new one.

Initial Training

Your first session can be to get your Caique to receive a treat from you. When it does, you can gently scratch its head as a reward. This is equivalent to gaining trust. When you can pet your Caique's head, you can move on to other things to teach such as getting it to step on your hand. The length of this initial training depends on the kind of bird you get: if it is a hand-fed chick, it will be immediate; if it is an untamed older bird, accepting a treat and petting can take a few weeks.

Advanced Training

Once the Caique trusts you and is no longer shy around you, you can train its behavior and teach it new tricks. As with any pet training, you need to remember that frequency of sessions and repetition of activities are vital. Your Caique can mimic most sounds, but they learn environmental sounds faster and better than human voices.

Again, don't be frustrated when your Caique cannot mimic as many human words as other parrots. This is important—never, ever punishes your Caique! You will effectively destroy whatever trust you've built when you do so and you will not get it to follow you or learn anything else.

Potential Behavior Problems

All birds have strengths and weaknesses. Training and playing with a Caique is lots of fun. They are smart birds and love to show off their tricks, especially when they see that they are being appreciated. However, they can be overstimulated—too much hopping, interaction and playing with toys can cause too much excitement that can turn into aggressiveness. An overly excited Caique can bite you or other birds around it. Only handle a Caique when he is calm. If you want to play with it, you can place it on a table top with toys or chew things then call it to go to you when it is in a calmer, more relaxed state.

Endearing Characteristics

Caiques are birds with a personality. It can mean a positive note to some and sound negative to others. You may enjoy an active, willful bird on one hand and resent an obstinate attitude on another. However you look at it, Caiques are generally playful and daring. They are always on the go, unlike other parrots who are content to sit calmly on a perch for a long time. They are quite exciting to watch, even when you are not playing with them. When they are not being aggressive or too excited, Caiques appear to be wearing fluffy pants, making their appearance quite endearing. Caiques are often known to be the kings of fascinating peculiar behavior. You will find yourself laughing at an excited Caique trying to hop in the air then falling across a flat surface—so much like a clown. Caiques also like to "surf" on towels or on people's hands and heads. They dive on the back of their head and slide on their back.

Chapter Nine: Decisions and Acquisition

A good time to start considering the responsibilities carried along with owning a caique bird should be determined really early on before acquisition. You don't want to be the one who has to give up a pet because of misconceptions. Caique birds are not only lovely to look at but they are amiable little fellas who like to be cuddled and favour cuddling their owners. Make it a point and look forward to many days and years of spending time, as you interact and play with your caique parrots. They require a tremendous amount of social interaction to thrive well in their shared life with you.

Should you be the sort who is kept away from home for extended hours of the day, make sure that you set up your caique parrot enclosure well and fit it with all the sundries they would need to keep themselves amused, occupied and engaged. Caique birds are generally independent and can be left alone for an extended period of time, but if given the choice, it would still much prefer your company to being left on its lonesome for longer than needed. For a sole bird, it is even more vital to set aside time for you and the bird to be visiting. It is irresponsible for anyone to acquire a pet and leave them to their own since birds that are not properly socialized will develop behavioural problems which could include attacking when startled, pecking, clawing, "bombing in" and loud screeching and squawking. These issues ruin the parrot's pet potential and create challenges to the owner, which would otherwise have been easily averted through the frequent socialization and interaction of you and your pet bird.

Patience and the openness to learning about your new caique companion will be the best thing you can do for your caique parrot. Caique parrots require the nurturing guidance and training provided for by their owners. Early socialization is an important stage that needs to be established early on in the caique parrots life, or as soon as the caique is big enough to be handled (in cases you are breeding them).

Last Minute Reminders

You want to look for a reputable breeder or bird dealer who cares about the birds under their care. They are the ones who not only answers your questions so that you are fully aware of what you are getting into, they would also have a few questions themselves to ask you about the facilities you have prepared for the birds, they would be concerned about the reasons for your desire to get a caique bird, and they are the ones who would not think twice about turning someone, who has ill-conceived ideas about owning and raising caique birds, away. When you do find a recently successful and upstanding caique parrot breeder you will want to inquire about a few important details.

The socialization the bird has been exposed to, and you also want to be observant about how the bird interacts. Is it skittish? Is it shy? Does it cower? Or does it willingly emerge from its enclosure, just as curious about you, as you are to it? Has the bird weaned off its mother? This is important because, no baby animal should be taken away from its mother until it has weaned off completely from the mother.

Removing a young chick from its mother too soon could result in behavioural problems and may cause stress and insecurity for the little feathered dude.

- Where was the bird obtained? How was it acquired by the establishment or person who is selling it?
- Has the bird been trained? Does it appear to be comfortable around human handlers?
- Has the bird been given the proper initial vaccinations it requires? Has it been administered the vaccine for polyomavirus?

Polyomavirus is a fatal infection which attacks a bird's body parts and organs at the same time. It is an infection that is commonly seen in captive birds that live in cages and enclosures, most especially captive parrots. It is the young parrots between 14 to 56 days who are usually affected by this deadly virus. This virus, once contracted by a bird, would take around 10-14 days for symptoms to begin showing. In other, more alarming cases, there are no signs to give indication to the virus in the bird, and this will lead to the bird's imminent death.

This virus lowers the bird's immune system, making them susceptible to other bacteria, viruses, parasites and fungi which ultimately may lead up to secondary infections and eventual death. This virus is typically contracted via the direct contact with an infected bird. Polyomavirus is also contracted from infected feces, from the air, from nest boxes, from dander, from incubator feather dust or, from a parent that is infected who ultimately passes on the virus to its hatchlings. There is no treatment for a bird that has contracted the polyomavirus.

Birds with polyomavirus infection could display symptoms such as a swollen belly, a sudden loss of appetite, regurgitation of food, vomiting, diarrhea, dehydration, weight loss, depression, abnormalities with their feathers (colouring and shedding of the feathers), excessive urination, and difficulty in breathing, hemorrhages or bleeding under the skin, restlessness, tremors and paralysis.

Make sure that you are given the proper supporting papers that indicate that the bird you are about to purchase has been vaccinated against this opportunistic virus that could rob you of a feathered, cuddly, playful buddy.

There is no treatment for this deadly virus, but there are ways to prevent this virus from occurring and this is something that has been stressed time and again throughout this informational booklet about caique parrot care - maintaining the cleanliness of enclosure is one sure way to avoid any illnesses from befalling your birds. Vaccine against this virus is given to young birds in double doses. The first dose is administered when the young chick is four weeks old and the second dose is administered about six to eight weeks after the initial administration of the vaccine.

Adult caique birds also get a double dose of the vaccine, with the second dose given about a month after the first one was given. Booster shots of the vaccine will then later be required on a yearly basis.

How to Spot a Healthy Caique

Caique parrots are some of the healthiest parrots around, so it is up to you as its owner/caregiver to maintain their wellness whilst under your care. Learn how to spot a healthy caique parrot because this initial measure of concern will be the hinge that will foretell the future wellness of the bird. It is important that you determine the history of the caique parrot you intend to take in so that you are not too surprised about possible eventualities that may rise. It is equally important that you pay frequent visits to the caique you intend to take home because it will give you better insight on its social behaviour and personality. You will also be able to witness the caique in its present environment, how it interacts with other birds, as well as its present owner/breeder, giving you valuable insight of how things will turn out when you take your caique bird home.

Determine the health and wellness of the bird before you take them home. Any signs of abnormalities in movement and mobility are a red flag. Signs of weakness and lethargy are another indication of a sick bird. A healthy caique parrots would be:

- attentive
- inquisitive
- spritely
- curious
- smart and clever
- sharp and intelligent
- able to support themselves with the little legs
- able to hop around without problems
- able to bear their weight whilst swinging on swings
- has no problem perching
- body is free of lumps, bumps and lesions
- is free of scales and scars on its body
- feathers are unruffled
- no bald spots anywhere on its body
- ears and eyes are absent of discharge
- beak is not ill formed, chipped or cracked

A healthy, well-rounded caique bird is curious as it is confident. They will display cautiousness to new surrounding but will soon be able to settle down given the proper space and time to get used to its new environment and human company. We hope that we have given you the important low-down on acquisition, adoption and care for the caique parrot. We wish you a long life of happy companionship with your new feathered buddy.

Chapter Ten: Conclusion and Summary

Every bird owner should learn to accept the good, the bad and the ugly when it comes to their pet birds. While birds are delightful and often magnificent, they are not perfect. The same is true for the Caique. It has become rather popular because of its remarkable appearance and its personality. Caiques are active birds, brave, spirited and often the comedian. They are mischief-makers and are often the clowns of the bird species. But they can also be very obstinate and beaky. Caiques are willful feathered creatures prone to aggression.

You need to be careful that they do not injure your other pet birds. However, Caiques are not all obstinate and mischievous. The general demeanor of these birds is friendliness and affection. In the wild, you will usually find Caiques in pairs or with their families or flocks.

In captivity, most Caiques love to interact with people and other birds. However, the black-headed Caiques are often aggressive, nippy, and grumpy with other birds. Since Caiques are generally sociable feathered beings, you should get a pair of them if you cannot allot a lot of time to just one pet. Caiques are moderately noisy birds—although they can't match up the noise of a cockatoo. You can teach them to cluck or whistle, but they are not very popular talking birds. Do not be frustrated when they cannot mimic everything you tell them.

Your Bird's Home

Caiques need a large environment because it is energetic. Even though your Caique is medium-sized, it will need a lot of space to move around, play, or fly. Get one that is appropriate for its size and behavior or choose the biggest housing that you can find the money for. Make sure the birdcage has ample space for food dishes, water containers, perches and playthings.

A minimum of 24 inches width x 24 inches length x 24 inches height is a good start for a cage. If you can get a bigger one, it will be better. A word of caution: the Caique is smart enough to find the weakness of a cage so make sure that you get one of high quality construction, so your bird won't destroy it or get out without your knowledge. Better to get one made of steel instead of wood so that it won't be easily destroyed and your bird's beak won't be too worn out.

You need to have horizontal bars for the Caiques to climb on as they love to move around. It is good to provide at least two bird perches: one for roosting and one near the food and water. Get perches made from willow, fruit trees or poplar branches. They are good for your Caiques' feet and beak, as they love to gnaw on the perches. Make sure that the cage is located away from drafts and harmful fumes. You can also cover your bird cage at night so that your Caique will have a sense of security.

Your Bird's Diet

Always have fresh food for your bird on a daily basis. Caiques love seeds, berries and fruits. You can give your Caiques a pelleted-base diet or seed mixture. You can also supplement their nourishment with vegetables. Get some Nutri-Berries to make eating more fun and balanced for them. Your Caique will love the adventure of foraging for its meals.

Here are some fresh vegetables you can give your pet: sweet corn, young dandelion greens, broccoli, carrots, beet greens, green peas, watercress, chickweed, endive, spinach leaves, sweet potatoes and unsprayed lettuce. For fruits, you can give bananas, plums, pears, raisins, apricots, apples and peaches. Never give them avocados—this fruit contains toxins that are lethal to birds!

As a treat, you can give walnuts to your Caiques occasionally. In a separate dish, you can provide it a calcium source such as a calcium block, a piece of cuttlebone, or gravel with oyster shell. Give your bird fresh water daily. You can also ask your avian vet about adding vitamin supplements to the bird's drinking water.

Your Bird's Playtime and Activities

Since Caiques are very active birds, you need to have a steady supply of toys for them to play with. As part of their energy-diet, get toys that are safe for them to pick on. Be watchful and take out ragged or disassembled toys to prevent your pet from getting hurt and replace them with new ones—which you may have to do often.

Some toys you can provide include wooden toys, link chains, bird swings, bird ladders, bells, climbing ropes and other bird toys. Rotate the bird toys for variety of activities. If you have a small cage, you will need to bring your Caique out so it can play and move around. It needs daily exercise to improve its physical well-being. You can get a playpen for this purpose. Your Caique needs to move around not just to be physically fit but to also be psychologically healthy. Moving around, chewing, climbing, pecking and playing with toys help prevent feather picking, screeching, and other forms of distress. Be very attentive whenever your Caique is out of its cage to avoid dangerous situations. Caiques are more vulnerable to polyomavirus and can affect important internal organs such as their liver, kidney, stomach and heart.

Your Bird's Bath and Grooming

Caiques are birds that love baths! Place a bath pan at the bottom of its cage and watch them dip themselves for a good wash. You can also give your pets a shower using a hand-held fine shower spray; just make sure the water is lukewarm. Since Caiques are active and aggressive, it is to their best interests that you keep their wings trimmed so they can't escape their cage and get lost and to discourage them from fighting other birds. You can also trim their beaks and claws.

Pet Bird Maintenance

As with any other pet, you need to provide clean environment for your bird. Make sure you clean the food dishes and water containers daily. The bird's toys and perches should be washed down once a week. You should also wash the floor of the bird cage every other week. Cleanliness results in good health.

Potential Problems

Caiques are easy to maintain as they are very robust birds. Some common signs that you need to watch out include: sneezing, discharge from nostrils, ruffled plumage, loss of appetite, cloudy eyes, resting with heads turned back and feces change. These can mean respiratory ailments, parrot fever, coccidiosis, intestinal influenza, or parasites. When you notice these symptoms, make sure to bring your ailing parrot to a veterinarian for correct diagnosis and immediate treatment.

Glossary of Bird Terms

Addled eggs - These eggs are not viable and will not hatch.

Afterfeather - A structure that projects from the shaft of the feather at the rim of the superior umbilicus.

Allopreening - An act of social grooming amongst birds, in which one bird preens the other or a pair of birds does so mutually.

alternate plumage - The plumage of birds displayed in time for courtship or a breeding season.

Altricial - hatchlings with their eyes closed, and are not capable of leaving the nest on its own, and relies on parents for food.

Alula - a bird's "thumb"

Anisodactylus - a bird foot which has three toes pointing forward and one toe pointing at the back

Anting - a behaviour when birds rub insects, typically ants, on their feathers and skin

Aviculture - captive breeding and raising of birds

Back- exterior area of a bird's upper parts between its mantle and rump

basic plumage - non-breeding plumage

Beak - bill or rostrum

beak trimming - the partial removal of the beak

Belly - the area beneath the chest of a bird

Billing - a tendency of mated pairs that strengthen couple bonding

bird banding - a tag attached to the leg of a bird to enable identification

bird strike - bird/s that impact with planes in flight

Body down - soft, down feathers underneath a birds outer feathers.

Breast - body part between throat and belly

breeding plumage - plumage displayed by birds during breeding season

Brood - offspring birds

brood patch - an area of bare skin well supplied with blood vessels at the surface, and facilitates the transfer of heat to the eggs

Call - bird vocalization intending to serve as warning alarm

Cloaca - birds expel waste from it; other mate by joining cloaca; females lay eggs from this region

contact call - to make known to their kind the location of a bird

Crissum - feathered area between the vent and the tail

cryptic plumage - plumage meant to camouflage birds

definitive plumage - plumage completely developed and fixed

Down - the softest of the birds feathers

Egg - where birds develop until hatched

egg incubation - act of warming the eggs to promote hatching

Eye-ring - visible ring of feathers surrounding a bird's eyes

Feather - distinct outer "garment" covering a birds' body

feather pecking - a behavioural problem when one bird repeatedly pecks at the feathers of another bird

Fledge - a young bird that completely develops its wing muscles and feather suitable for flight

Fledgling - the period when a completely formed young bird ventures out of the nest and learns to take flight

Flight - the act of soaring in the air with the use of wings

Gizzard - specialized stomach organ found in the digestive tract of some birds used to grind up food and aided with grit or stone particles

Gleaning - a bird strategy used to catch insect prey

Grooming - the act of preening and self-cleaning

Iris - coloured outer ring surrounding birds' pupil

Lek - male aggression when in competition for the attention of a female

Mantle - front area of a bird's upper portion found between nape and top back

Migration - seasonal movement of birds

Morph - a polymorphic plumage colour variance between the same species

Moult - a periodic shedding and replacement of feathers

Nail - hard tissue at the tip of a bird's beak

Nares - two holes leading to the nasal cavities in the bird's skull

Nest - a bird's lair and home; where a female lays eggs and roosts

Over-brooding - a phenomenon when birds continue to brood eggs not likely to hatch

Passerine - any bird of the order Passeriformes

Pinioning - the removal of the joint of a bird's wing farthest from the body preventing flight

Plumage - refers to feathers covering a bird as well as pattern, colour and arrangement of feathers

Plumeology - the study of feathers

---

pre-alternate moult - also known as the prenuptial moult when basic plumage is shed to make way for nuptial plumage

prebasic moult - moult birds go through after breeding season

Precocial - young birds that after hatched has their eyes open

Preening - grooming od feathers in birds

Quill - the main stem of a feather where all structures branch from

Resident - a non-migratory bird

rictal bristles stiff, tapering feathers around the eyes of some birds

Rosette - a found at the corners of the beaks of some birds. A fleshy rosette area

Rump - area of a bird's body between the end of the back and the base of the tail

sexual dimorphism - common occurrence amongst birds in which males and females of a similar sort display different character traits

Song - bird vocalization associated with courtship

Speculum - A patch of typically bright coloured feathers, often iridescent

Sternum - bird's breastbone

Syrinx - the vocal organs of birds

Tail streamers - narrow tips of the tail of some birds

Talon - claw of bird of prey

Teleoptiles - feathers of an adult bird

Throat - body area located between the chin and the upper part of the breast

Thigh - body part between knee and trunk of the bird's body

Vent - the outer opening of the cloaca

Wings - The bird's forelimbs that are the essential to flight

Wingspan - distance between wings from one wing tip to the other

Index

A

accessories..14, 44, 45, 84, 130, 140, 148

Asymptomatic...123, 125, 126

Aviary..56, 57

B

behavior..11, 40, 41, 137

breeder...13,49,53,54,55,82,110,114,116

breeding............................. 11, 12, 109, 110, 111, 112, 113, 114, 115, 141, 149

brooding..114

C

cage...................................140, 43, 44, 45, 47, 84, 85, 86, 87, 88, 89, 92, 99, 130, 137, 140, 146

calcium...100, 101, 141

CITES...50,51,52

clutch..11, 54, 111, 113, 114, 142

cost 39, 40, 43, 44, 45, 46, 47, 48

cyanosis...128

cuttlebone...100, 140, 141

D

diagnosis .... 126, 129, 131,133, 134, 135 diet 12, 46, 54, 89, 90, 93, 94, 95, 99, 100, 130, 139, 141, 150

diseases 13, 52, 94, 99, 113, 119, 120, 121, 135

dishes..44, 88, 89, 130, 140, 148

DNA..11, 110, 131, 132

droppings...89, 113, 136

E

E-Coli........................11, 12, 99, 100, 111, 113, 114, 115, 139, 142

eggs...42, 85, 113, 127, 130

environment 17,37,39,44,69,70,72,82

eyes...20, 21, 82, 121, 125, 128, 137

F

family...10, 12, 14, 139

feather...............................9, 10, 40, 42, 82, 91, 99, 131, 136, 137

feeding...44, 46, 93, 94, 95, 130

female...11, 109, 110, 111, 114, 142

food.....................46, 47, 48, 84, 86, 88, 89, 90, 94, 102, 136, 140, 141, 142, 150

fruits...46, 90, 93, 97, 99, 102, 130, 141

G

genus...16, 17, 18, 25, 26, 27, 28, 29

Great Britain...50, 52, 53, 78, 146, 147

grooming...43, 45, 91, 106, 107, 140

H

habitat...12, 27, 85, 137, 139

handling 91, 103

hatching 114, 142

health...52, 54, 82, 86, 88, 89, 120, 123, 131, 135, 137

history 7,23,55

hygiene...45, 91

I

illness..95, 121, 123, 127, 135

immune system...95, 122, 123, 127, 130

incubation...11, 12, 111, 114, 115, 139, 142

infection............120, 121, 122, 123, 124, 125, 128, 129, 132, 133, 134, 135, 137

initial costs...43

L

lay...142

license...52

lifespan...2, 11, 12, 139

longevity..82

M

male...109, 110

mating...111

maturity 11, 12, 110, 111, 114, 139, 142

N

nails..91, 103, 106, 107, 130, 131

nest... 111, 113, 114, 115, 140, 142

nesting..113, 114

nutrients..89, 90, 93, 94, 95

nutritional...46, 93, 94, 141

needs.....................................45, 46, 47, 84, 85, 86, 88, 91, 94, 99, 131

O

oil..91, 143

order...12, 85, 94, 112, 139

P

Pacheco's Disease...126

parrots.........................2, 3, 8, 9, 11, 42, 45, 47, 90, 92, 94, 97, 102

PBFD virus...130

pellet...46, 89, 90, 94, 95, 99, 140

perches................................44, 86, 88, 89, 130, 140, 142, 143

permit...49, 51, 52

pet store...13, 45, 46, 53, 54, 89, 107

prevention...119, 130, 132, 137

Psittacosis...125, 126

Q

quick..12, 14, 15, 18, 105

R

reproduction..11, 110, 111, 113

respiratory................................91, 121, 122, 125, 127, 128, 129, 133, 137, 143

S

seeds..................11, 12, 46, 89, 90, 93, 94, 96, 97, 103, 130, 139, 141, 143, 150

seed mix...89, 140, 141

sexing...11, 110, 141

sexually dimorphic...11, 12, 110, 139, 141

species..............................9, 13, 106, 115, 120, 124, 127, 129, 130, 142

symptoms.................119, 120, 121, 122, 123, 124, 125, 126, 127, 131, 133, 134

T

taming...104

training...102, 103, 105, 106, 143

temperature 91, 92, 111, 140

toys...35, 43, 44, 45, 47, 89, 140, 142, 148

Treats...46, 90, 102

treatment...............................47, 101, 120, 121, 122, 124, 129, 130, 132, 134

types.............................9, 14, 18, 35, 36, 37, 39, 41, 42, 47, 88, 90, 94, 141

U

United States..13, 26, 27, 50, 51, 52, 55, 116, 146

V

vegetables...46, 90, 95, 99, 130, 141, 127

ventilation...127

veterinarian 91, 97, 99, 107, 108, 135, 137, 143

virus. 120, 121, 122, 123, 124, 126, 127, 131, 132

W

water...86, 87, 88, 89, 90, 91, 101

wild 37, 42, 50, 88, 93, 94, 106, 113

wingspan...11, 12, 19, 20, 21, 25, 28, 31, 32

Photo Credits

References

Caique – Good Bird Inc.

http://www.goodbirdinc.com/parrot-profiles-caique.html

Caiques –The Spruce

https://www.thespruce.com/caiques-390505

Caique – Wikipedia.org

https://en.wikipedia.org/wiki/Caique

Caique as Pets – BeautyofBirds.com

https://www.beautyofbirds.com/caiquesaspets.html

Caique Breeding & Egg Laying – ShadyPines.com

http://shadypines.com/caique-breeding.htm

Caique Care: Bird Information and Bird Care For Caique
Birds – Animal – World.com

http://animal-
world.com/encyclo/birds/Caiques/CaiquesProfile.htm

Caiques (Pionites) Species Profile: Black – headed and White
– Bellied Caiques – PetEducation.com

http://www.peteducation.com/article.cfm?c=15+1840&aid=23
43

Foods Caiques Eat in the Wild – CaiqueSite.com

http://caiquesite.com/foods/foods_eaten_in_wild.htm

Ideal Temperature Ranges For Parrots – Petcha.com

https://www.petcha.com/ideal-temperature-ranges-for-parrots/

Notes of a Fanatic Hobby Caique Breeder – CaiqueSite.com

http://caiquesite.com/published%20articles/fanatic_hobby_breeder.htm

Parrot and Kids: A Good Mix? Should I Get My Child a Pet Parrot?

https://www.thespruce.com/parrot-and-kids-a-good-mix-390727

Polyomavirus in Birds – Petmd.com

https://www.petmd.com/bird/conditions/neurological/c_bd_Polyomavirus

The Unique Caique – Petcha.com

https://www.petcha.com/the-unique-caique/

Feeding Baby
Cynthia Cherry
978-1941070000

Axolotl
Lolly Brown
978-0989658430

Dysautonomia, POTS
Syndrome
Frederick Earlstein
978-0989658485

Degenerative Disc
Disease Explained
Frederick Earlstein
978-0989658485

Sinusitis, Hay Fever,
Allergic Rhinitis Explained
Frederick Earlstein
978-1941070024

Wicca
Riley Star
978-1941070130

Zombie Apocalypse
Rex Cutty
978-1941070154

Capybara
Lolly Brown
978-1941070062

Eels As Pets
Lolly Brown
978-1941070167

Scabies and Lice Explained
Frederick Earlstein
978-1941070017

Saltwater Fish As Pets
Lolly Brown
978-0989658461

Torticollis Explained
Frederick Earlstein
978-1941070055

Kennel Cough
Lolly Brown
978-0989658409

Physiotherapist, Physical
Therapist
Christopher Wright
978-0989658492

Rats, Mice, and Dormice
As Pets
Lolly Brown
978-1941070079

Wallaby and Wallaroo Care
Lolly Brown
978-1941070031

Bodybuilding Supplements
Explained
Jon Shelton
978-1941070239

Demonology
Riley Star
978-19401070314

Pigeon Racing
Lolly Brown
978-1941070307

Dwarf Hamster
Lolly Brown
978-1941070390

Cryptozoology
Rex Cutty
978-1941070406

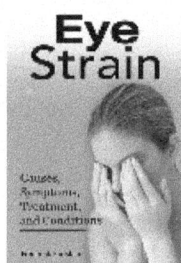

Eye Strain
Frederick Earlstein
978-1941070369

Inez The Miniature Elephant
Asher Ray
978-1941070353

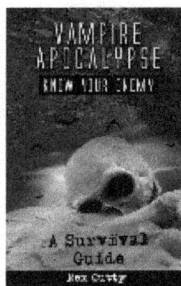

Vampire Apocalypse
Rex Cutty
978-1941070321